Pages From My Parallel

Stories between Silences

Dr. Nirmala Khess

BookLeaf Publishing

India | USA | UK

Made with ❤ on the BookLeaf Publishing Platform

www.bookleafpub.in

www.bookleafpub.com

Dedication

I dedicate this book to my beloved family and my loved ones. I thank to the almighty whose grace and inspiration have guided me every step of the way.

With heartfelt gratitude,

Dr. Nirmala Khess

Preface

Pages from My Parallel: Stories Between Silences is a collection born from the spaces that words often fail to fill. Each piece reflects a fragment of my journey, moments of innocence, loss, love, growth, and quiet realisations that shaped who I am today. These stories and poems are not just recollections but reflections of emotions that once lingered between the lines of everyday life.

Through these pages, I wanted to capture the beauty of the ordinary, the scent of childhood memories, the ache of goodbyes, the comfort of moonlight conversations, and the strength that comes from simply being. Some pieces are raw, some are tender, and some are whispers of the soul trying to make peace with itself.

This collection is not just mine; it belongs to anyone who has ever felt too much, stayed quiet when words were too heavy, or found healing in their solitude. May these stories remind you that silence too has a voice; gentle, powerful, and endlessly human.

Acknowledgements

First and foremost, I bow in gratitude to the Almighty, whose guiding hand and grace have lit my path through every step of this journey. Without His strength, wisdom, and quiet presence, these pages would have remained unwritten.

This book would not have been possible without the love, encouragement, and support of those who have walked beside me through different chapters of life. I am deeply thankful to my family for their unwavering faith in me, for their patience, and for believing in my dreams even when I hesitated. To my friends, who filled my days with laughter, warmth, and countless memories, thank you for inspiring the stories that breathe within these pages.

My heartfelt appreciation goes to everyone who encouraged me to keep writing and believed in the power of my words. Your kindness reminded me that even silence has meaning when shared with understanding hearts.

Above all, I thank the Lord for being my constant source of strength and peace, for turning every trial into a lesson and every silence into a story.

1. Oh, My Childhood Days

The age was golden, the streets wore light,
Days bathed in joy, and stars in the night.
No weight of future, no fear of tomorrow,
Just laughter and dreams, untouched by sorrow.
Thoughts soaked in culture, gentle and kind,
No room for envy in my tender mind.
The face I adored, my morning sun,
Was always my mother, my only one.
To be like her, my truest aim,
With hands that healed and heart aflame.
And oh, my aunt! So graceful, so grand,
With dazzling clothes and sandals so glam.
The first man I loved with innocent pride,
Was my father, forever by my side.
My brother, the one I called my friend,
Our bond too true to break or bend.
In class, I was the chatter queen,
With stories bright and mischief seen.
The "Pooh" of the era, bold and sweet,
With joy and jokes, none could compete.

My friends were gems, rare and true,
To them, my heart I always knew.
We shared our secrets, hopes, and fears,
Laughed through days, cried happy tears.
Oh! What a childhood, pure and bright,
A canvas painted in morning light.
It cannot return, it cannot repeat,
But lives in my soul, forever sweet.

2. My Superhero

What Should I Name You?
A superhero... or an angel true,
I've known you since my world first grew,
Just a year behind, you took your part,
Already guarding my tiny heart.

You were the first to call me my baby,
And soon the world echoed that sweet maybe.
We grew together, step by step,
And best of friends, the bond we kept.

Our thread grew strong with time's soft flow,
Though as adults, we drifted so.
We meet less often, hardly now,
No more fights, yet time knows how.

Though we don't laugh like days before,
You are still my peace, my core.
My superhero, my truest friend,
Forever my elder brother, till the end.

3. Back to Those Days

I had a flashback, sweet and clear,
Of days with mom, dad, and dada near.
Christmas lights and New Year cheer,
Birthdays filled with love sincere.

Back then, my world was safe and small,
Their arms my heaven, I had it all.
Laughter echoed, love overflowed,
Life was warm, no heavy load.

But now adulthood feels so cold,
Dreams feel distant, joy seems old.
I miss the child I used to be,
Everyone's baby, loved endlessly.

Oh, to return, to run back in time,
Where life was simple, and all was fine.
For in their hearts, I found my place,
A world of love, a warm embrace.

Though I can't go back, I'll hold on tight,
To those golden days, my heart's delight.
And maybe in memories, I'll find my way,
To keep their love alive today.

4. Strawberry's Life

Strawberries red, with hearts so bright,
Some are sweet and full of light.
Some are sour, a little wild,
But still, they make the journey worthwhile.
The sweet one's shine, so soft, so pure,
A taste of joy, calm and sure.
The sour one's sting, they make you frown,
But cook them slow, they wear a crown.
In bubbling pots, with sugar's grace,
They find their shine, they find their place.
From sharp beginnings, thick and bold,
They turn to jam as stories told.
So, let's grow through every stage,
Through every smile and every rage.
Like strawberries, both sweet and tart,
Each one blooms with a different heart.

5. I Am a Woman

I am a woman, bold and free,
Yet burdened by what the world sees in me.
Born to a life where struggles began,
Carrying dreams yet raised as a man.

A daughter, a sister, a student bright,
An idol they wished would shine in light.
But behind the glow, the battles grew,
Sacrifices made, yet nobody knew.

Success came knocking, and I took my flight,
Yet my childhood dreams stayed out of sight.
Now I live them, now I soar,
Yet my heart whispers, it longs for more.

A soul to cherish, a hand to hold,
A love that's gentle, strong, and bold.
Not just settled, but steady and true,
To heal the scars life etched in view.

But at this time, I stand alone,
A fate the world has cruelly sewn.
Not for lack of love or grace,
But for the standards I refuse to chase.

Now the whispers turn to cries,
"Marry soon!" a fate unwise.
As if my worth, my battles won,
Mean nothing until I belong to one.

And yet I crave, not wealth or gold,
But arms where peace is mine to hold.
A place to breathe, to rest my mind,
A love so pure, so unconfined.

Being a woman is not so light,
A journey long, a fearless fight.
Yet through the storms, I stand so proud,
A woman strong, fierce, and unbowed.

6. My Everyday Prayer

Lord, you are the father,
And You are the Saviour,
You hold the power over every creature on earth,
And command the winds that circle its worth.
I praise you with all my heart and soul,
I sing to you, even in my tears and fall,
For you are my peace, my strength, and my world.

Lord, you are the father,
And you are the Saviour,
Before I came into my mother's womb, you knew me,
Before I opened my eyes, you planned the path for me.
I trust you with all my heart and soul,
I seek you even when the night is dark and long,
For your light alone keeps me strong.

Lord, you are the father,
And you are the Saviour,
There are times when I lose all hope,
When storms inside me begin to choke.

There are times I can't see the way,
And feel so lost, with no words to pray.
Then your voice alone comforts me,
Your teachings show the way out of nowhere,
Your love gives me hope and courage to bear,
And your mercy calms the storm within me.

Lord, you are the father,
And you are the Saviour,
Forever I'll trust, forever I'll praise,
For Your grace follows all my days.

7. A Love Letter to the Lord

Whenever the sun begins to rise,
I fear the day, I close my eyes.
The battle starts within my mind,
Peace feels distant, hard to find.

My heart grows weak, my courage fades,
Anxiety builds its silent cage.
But You, my Lord, are always near,
Your whisper cuts through every fear.

You helped young David stand so tall,
To face Goliath and not fall.
You shut the lions' hungry jaws,
And saved dear Daniel without pause.

You move the mountains, calm the seas,
You walk the valleys deep with me.
You are the Shepherd, kind and true,
Each wandering soul returns to You.

Your words bring peace, your love brings light,
You turn my darkness into sight.
My trembling heart finds rest in you,
As tears fall soft like morning dew.

And in that peace, I see it clear,
Each time I fall, you draw me near.
Unlike the world that fades away,
I fall in love with you each day.

8. A winter Evening

A winter evening, calm and bright,
I stood and watched the fading light.
The sun went down, the sky turned red,
Soft and quiet, the day had fled.

The air was cold, the world was still,
The sunset wrapped me in its will.
A peaceful moment, warm and near,
A gentle end to the day, so clear.

9. Jhal Murhi Memories

Jhal Murhi in my hand, simple and sweet,
A taste of Bengal on a busy street.
On trains, in crowds, in moments small,
It was there with me, through it all.

Crunchy bites, spicy and warm,
Through happy days and life's storm.
Now each bite brings memories near,
The taste of past, forever dear.

10. Girls Trip

One of the trips I had on my bucket list,
With my girls, it's too good to resist.
We eat together, laugh till late,
Dress up, click pics, it feels so great.

We share our blush, our lipstick too,
Fix each other's hair and shoe.
Sometimes we fight over who will pay,
But hug it out the very next day.

We shop for weeks, plan every spot,
We talk for hours, yes, we talk a lot.
From sunrise chats to midnight songs,
With my girls, the world feels strong.

It's not just travel, it's pure delight,
A memory that feels so right.
Girls trip magic is simple and true,
Made of love and laughter, too.

11. The Proposal

In the depths, I fall for you,
Yearning to make you my destiny, too.
I dream of you, my everything,
Though I know not all, my heart does sing.

Tears fall as I think of you,
Your presence fills my day anew.
To shower you with love so grand,
To celebrate with hand in hand.

Together we'll grow, side by side,
Walking in faith, with love as our guide.
In short, my darling, hear this plea,
I love you deeply, endlessly.

12. Moon and You

The moon peeks through the whispering trees,
Its silver light rides on the breeze.
It paints the lake in softest hue,
A quiet world that dreams of you.

The stars lean close, the night turns slow,
Beneath the sky's enchanted glow.
Your hand in mine, so warm, so true,
The moon above, and me with you.

The flowers hush, the owls take flight,
The world wrapped up in velvet night.
No need for words, just hearts that knew,
The night was made for me and you.

The moon will fade, the sun will rise,
But love still lingers in the skies.
In every leaf, in drops of dew,
The moon remembers me and you.

13. I Was the Poem He Never Read

I was written
in margins of moments
soft silence between his questions,
and the way my hands paused
just before reaching out.

I folded metaphors
into the way I laughed at his stories,
into the tea I brewed just right,
into the way I waited
without asking.

He skimmed
the title of me,
liked the font,
maybe the cover,
but never turned the page.

He didn't see

the ink that ran from my wrists
when I said, I'm okay,
or the stanza hidden in my sighs
when the room went quiet.

I loved him in verses,
long, unrhymed
but full of rhythm.
He loved headlines,
not footnotes.

So I closed the book.
Not out of spite,
but to stop bleeding ink
for someone who only
reads to forget.

And somewhere,
between unspoken words
and unopened chapters,
I became
the poem he never read.

14. The Sound of the Sea

Have you ever heard the sea,
The soft waves calling quietly?
Not the crash, but the gentle sound,
Where peace and calm are always found.

The breeze that moves across the shore,
Whispers things not said before.
The foam that dances, white and light,
Shines like stars in the moonlit night.

Each wave comes close, then slips away,
Like the sea has something to say.
It tells of time, of dreams once deep,
Of secrets that the waters keep.

If you sit and simply hear,
The world feels soft, the heart feels clear.
For in its song, both wild and free,
Lives in the peace of the endless sea.

15. Where Do I Go?

I have been to the past, I've seen the days gone,
I've looked at the future, where new things come on.
I saw the year 2023 fly by,
And even saw the future 2052[1] stand by.

But I never stayed in the time called now,
It feels too heavy somehow.

I love the spring with flowers so bright,
And I wait for winter, cold and white.
But summer is something I don't enjoy,
The heat takes away the simple joy.

Green trees make me feel calm and free,
But dry, falling leaves don't comfort me.
We all want colours, smiles, and light,
But try to run from the hard and the fight.

The future can scare us, so far and unknown,
The past can hurt when we're all alone.

So where do I go, where do I begin?
When time feels too thick to let me in?

Maybe the present is where I should be,
Right here, right now, just being me.

[1] *Dreams of 2052*

16. Stuck in Between

The worst is being stuck midway,
Can't move ahead, can't walk away.
Can't give up, yet can't begin,
This restless way I hold within.

Life's a gamble, that's the game,
A lucky strike, you rise to fame.
Miss the mark, you lose it all,
And still, I stand, afraid to fall.

Yes, I know, it's win or lose,
But what about the ones who choose
To wait between the rise and fall,
Where nothing moves, just silence calls?

Waiting... for the storm to fade,
For light to break this endless shade.
For winds to shift, for skies to clear,
For joy to drown this aching fear.

Waiting for a heart at peace,
For all the noise inside to cease.
For just one sign, a door, a key,
To set this tired spirit free.

I'm done with feeling stuck and small,
No rise, no rest, no risk at all.
Want to escape, but still I stay,
Held by hope and disarray.

Only the Lord can see me through,
But what to do when even you
Feel distant in this in-between,
Where dreams grow dim and faith turns lean.

17. A Blur Memory

A blur memory of my first love,
A decade has gone since we met.
Petals fell and bells rang,
A world so bright, I can't forget.

My heart would dance, my cheeks would smile,
Time felt perfect for a while.
The world around us glowed and gleamed,
Life was sweeter than I dreamed.

A decade passed, and we drifted apart,
Like Moon and Sun, never to start.
The pain of him, a soulless man,
A fish out of water lost its span.

My heart would ache, my mind said "no,"
Memories came, a ceaseless flow.
I tried to forget, I tried to flee,
But the more I ran, the more I'd see.

Years have passed, and I have learned,
He's a part of me, for which I've yearned.
The pain has dulled, the harsh times fade,
The smiles we shared still softly stay.

I neither miss him nor feel the lack,
I neither love him nor turn back.
I forgive him now, and thank him too,
For teaching me what time can do.

Slowly I trust, slowly I see,
The meaning of moving on can be.
The heart heals, the soul grows strong,
And life flows gently, like a song.

18. The Irony of Life

Giving up is easy,
But holding on is hard.
Comfort feels gentle,
While struggle leaves scars.

We choose delay over doing,
The smooth over the rough.
We flee from the future,
Afraid to be tough.

Is this the irony of life?
Or is this how we meant to behave?

19. When Anxiety Wakes Me

I woke up with trembling in my chest,
Dreams of worry stole my rest.
The past still whispers, the future cries,
And fear paints clouds across my skies.

I ranted, "Lord, how long must I stay,
In dreams that steal my peace away?
How long must I pretend to be strong,
When my spirit feels so wrong?"

Then softly, you called my name,
Through the silence, through my shame:
"Everything has its time, my dear,
Under heaven, no need for fear.

Be strong and brave, don't be dismayed,
For I am with you, unafraid.
Wherever you go, I walk beside,
My love for you will never hide."

Oh Lord, how could I not adore,
The One who loves me evermore?
You never forsake me, not a day,
You calm my storms and light my way.

In every tear, you've been my song,
In every weakness, you've made me strong.
So here I stand, with heart renewed,
I love You, Lord, forever true.

20. The Art of Letting the Ache Breathe

The ache of voidness, it's real, it stays,
A hollow pain that shadows days.
Like a silent wind, it chills the bone,
I begged it to pass, but the air stood stone.

It would not move, it would not go,
Just lingered deep, so cold, so slow.
I dreamed of fleeing, drifting wide,
But dreams themselves got lost inside.

I tried to smother it with light,
With noise, with screens, with endless night.
But still it bloomed where shadows lie,
It rooted deep behind my sigh.

So, I at last unclenched my fist,
No longer fought what would persist.
No more escape, no urge to hide
I let the window swing open wide.

Perhaps this ache was sent to stay,
To teach, to shape, to mark the way.
And now I wear it in my skin
Not gone, not healed, but known within.

21. She's Becoming

She turned thirty,
and life flipped the script.
No more soft landings,
just tightrope trips.
No more picking colours for dresses to wear,
now it's "choose right" or beware.

It isn't just love,
It's a forever talk,
one wrong step,
And you change your walk.
Hearts on the line,
and futures too,
not just hers,
But the circle she knew.

They ask, "Why so picky?"
She bites her tongue,
Cause choosing wrong isn't easily undone.
She's not afraid to be alone in a room,

She's afraid of planting roots
that bloom into doom.

And then,
the weight talk starts to roll.
Every "Hey, you're chubby"
cuts a hole.
Like softness is a shame,
Like curves are crime,
But she carries the weight
of a thousand minds.

Anxiety's a shadow
that hugs her tight,
turns quiet days
into mental fights.
Right or wrong,
The war never ends,
and peace feels distant,
just out of hands.

But no, she doesn't want to be chosen
like grapes off a vine,
She wants to be seen,
fully, divine.
Not fixed, not moulded,
not picked apart,

just loved loud
with an open heart.

She wants mornings that start
with a calm, sweet light,
a partner who stays
when things aren't right.
And a mirror that smiles
without judgment in glass,
where she nods and says,
"Damn, I'm badass."

So, if you see her
walking through storms,
know this isn't breaking
This is her form.
She's not falling,
she's shedding skin.
Not ending,
just about to begin.